What are clouds?

Clouds are made up of lots of very small droplets of liquid. They float up in the sky.

Clouds are normally white, but they can look grey (/graɪ/), or even red and pink at sunset or sunrise.

What are the different sorts of clouds?

There are ten main sorts of clouds. They have different names depending on their shape and on where in the sky they are found (high up, in the middle or low down).

Clouds all have long names that come from Latin.

A cloudy sky is often said to bring rain, but in fact only two sorts of clouds normally bring rain. Carry on reading to see which ones...

Cirrus (/**si**rus/) clouds are thin and wispy. They look like fur or cotton wool, and they are seen high up in the sky. These thin clouds never bring rain.

These clouds can be made from the contrails left in the sky when a plane has flown by.

contrails

Cirrocumulus (/siroacuemuelus/) are made up of lots of little fluffy clouds clumped together high up in the sky.

clouds

Sometimes it is said that these sorts of clouds look like fish scales.

What do you think?

fish scales

Cirrostratus (/siroa**strah**tus/) clouds are light and very thin indeed.

3

rainbow ring

Sometimes, this sort of cloud forms a white or rainbow ring around the Sun or the Moon.

This ring is called a halo (/**hai**loa/).

Cumulonimbus (/cuemueloanimbus/) clouds are one of only two sorts of clouds that bring rain. They are tall, towering clouds that often bring thunder, lightning and hail, too.

These clouds can look like a mountain in the sky, and they often have a flat top and bottom.

Nimbostratus (/nimboa**strah**tus/) clouds are thick, dark layers of cloud. They often bring rain or snow, but never hail or thunder and lightning.

falling rain

Clouds like these are so thick that they block out much of the sunlight.

Altostratus (/altoa**strah**tus/) are big, thin sheets of cloud spread out across the sky. They sometimes turn into rain clouds.

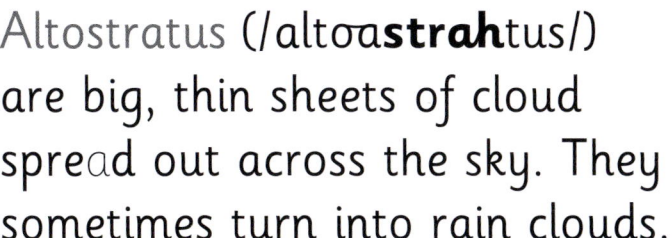

6

Often the Sun cannot make shadows when there are a lot of these clouds in the sky.

Altocumulus (/altoa**cue**muelus/) are normally found all clumped together in the middle of the sky.

Sometimes these clouds form strips or lines. When this happens, they are called cloud streets!

cloud streets

Stratocumulus

(/stratoacuemuelus/) clouds are low in the sky. They can be many different shapes.

8

Sometimes, these clouds can look like waves in the sky. These are called asperitas clouds.

Cumulus (/**cue**muelus/) are small, fluffy clouds that float low in the sky. Sometimes, these clouds can grow into storm clouds.

9

These clouds can form stripes, or cloud streets, in the sky as well.

Stratus (/**strah**tus/) clouds are blankets of cloud that sit very close to the ground.

10

Sometimes, these clouds sit so low in the sky that they touch the ground!

13

Clouds can form a lot of odd shapes.

Sometimes a cloud can form lumpy, bumpy shapes like this at the bottom. These are called mammatus clouds. They are a sort of thunderstorm cloud.

These oddly-shaped clouds often form around mountains. Sometimes it is said that these clouds look like UFOs or hats.

What does this cloud look like to you?

Believe it or not, fog is a sort of cloud too. When clouds sit on the ground, we call it fog or mist. So remember, when you are walking in the fog, you are in fact walking in the middle of a cloud!

Fog can make things look spooky.